Today's Tejano Heroes

Today's Tejano Heroes

SAMMYE MUNSON

EAKIN PRESS Austin, Texas

FIRST EDITION

Copyright © 2000
By Sammye Munson

Published in the United States of America
By Eakin Press
A Division of Sunbelt Media, Inc.
P.O. Drawer 90159 🖂 Austin, Texas 78709-0159
email: eakinpub@sig.net
💻 website: www.eakinpress.com 💻

ALL RIGHTS RESERVED.

1 2 3 4 5 6 7 8 9

1-57168-328-3

Library of Congress Cataloging-in-Publication Data

Munson, Sammye.
    Today's Tejano heroes / by Sammye Munson.
       p.   cm.
    Includes bibliographical references and index.
    Summary: Examines the accomplishments and contributions of fifteen contemporary Hispanics with a strong Texas connection, including Vikki Carr, Dan Morales, and Vicente Villa.
    ISBN 1-57168-328-3
    1. Mexican Americans--Texas Biography. 2. Heroes--Texas Biography. 3. Texas Biography. [1. Mexican Americans--Texas. 2. Texas Biography.] I. Title.
F395.M5M88   2000
920'.00926872073--dc21
                                                   99-36015
                                                      CIP

*Dedicated to the memory of my late parents,
Margaret and Sam McLelland,
who gave me the love
of books and reading.*

Contents

Introduction   vii

IRMA AGUILAR   1
    Nurse and Educator
VIKKI CARR   5
    Entertainer
HECTOR GALAN   10
    Filmmaker
CARMEN LOMAS GARZA   15
    Artist and Writer
ELIGIO (KIKA) DE LA GARZA   19
    United States Congressman
TISH HINOJOSA   24
    Musician and Folksinger
LUIS JIMÉNEZ   30
    Sculptor
LINDA SAGARNAGA MAGILL   35
    Physician
PAT MORA   40
    Writer and Teacher
DAN MORALES   46
    Attorney General of Texas
GUADALUPE QUINTANILLA   52
    Writer and Educator
HILDA TAGLE   57
    United States Federal Judge

FRANK TEJEDA 61
  United States Congressman
JESSE TREVIÑO 65
  Artist
VICENTE VILLA 70
  Scientist and Professor
JUDITH ZAFFIRINI 76
  Texas Senator

Bibliography 81

Introduction

Tejanos (tay **hah** nos) lived in Texas long before Texas was a state. A *Tejano* is a Mexican-American with roots in Texas. For many years Texas was part of Mexico. Spanish was the main language. Mexican-Americans fought to free Texas from Mexico's rule, then helped set up the first government.

Mexican-Americans started the first churches, schools, and ranches in Texas. They have been contributing to our state for many years. In my first book, *Our Tejano Heroes,* I wrote about early heroes such as Lorenzo De Zavala, the Seguins, Antonio Navarro, and Emma Tenayuca. This book emphasizes outstanding individuals who have contributed to our state in the twentieth century and will continue to do so in the twenty-first century. We owe each a debt of gratitude for his or her leadership and sacrifices.

One of the heroes in this book is Jesse Treviño, the artist who lost his right hand in the jungles of Vietnam, then learned to paint with his left hand. Kika de la Garza gave fifty years of his life to govern our state and nation as a lawmaker. Dr. Guadalupe Quintanilla, despite early discouragement, never gave up her desire for education, earned a doctorate, and became a college professor. Hilda Tagle is the first woman to be a federal judge in Texas.

All of these individuals overcame hardships, prejudice, and sometimes poverty to become leaders in their fields.

It is not possible to include all the outstanding Mexican Americans who have made a real difference in our state. Those in this book are a few of the many who have achieved so much in the fields of art, science, music, entertainment, literature, and government. We are grateful for their lives and their work.

Irma Aguilar
NURSE AND EDUCATOR

"I would go to the library, a shy Mexican girl, almost afraid to touch the books. The librarian, Helen Hunt, was kind to me. She asked me if I wanted her help in choosing a book.

"I nodded and she handed me a copy of *Little Women*. I checked the book out and began reading it at once. This happened over and over. Each time I went to the library, Miss Hunt would have another wonderful book for me to read. It might be *Huckleberry Finn, Black Beauty,* or another of the children's classics. She opened up the world of reading to me. And I've never stopped reading. I didn't realize the gift Miss Hunt gave me until I was in college."

This happened in Marfa, Texas, where Irma Aguilar grew up. She developed curiosity about many things and has spent her life learning new ideas. She likes to share her knowledge with others and spends part of her time teaching nurses new concepts and procedures in medicine.

This pursuit of knowledge coupled with the ability to study led to her earning a doctorate degree in nursing. She is also certified as a nurse practitioner. During her training she taught at Texas Tech University Health Sciences Center School of Nursing in Odessa. All the

Irma Aguilar
—*Courtesy of Irma Aguilar*

while undertaking this task, she commuted from Odessa to Dallas to do research at the University of Texas Medical Center. Helping with her expenses as she studied were funds from the American Nurses Association Ethnic Minority Program.

Growing up, Irma Aguilar's family was poor, but she did not feel deprived or realize that they were victims of poverty. Although her parents divorced when she was ten, her mother gave her strong values and morals.

Another peson who greatly influenced her and gave her confidence was her high school English teacher, Emma Lou Howard. She encouraged Irma to enter a writing contest and compete with students from other schools. When Irma won third place, her teacher praised her.

"Irma, you're special," she said.

And Irma believed her. She felt she could achieve almost any goal she set for herself. And she has set many goals over the years. In far West Texas where the wind often blows dust over the prairies, Irma's ambition to be a nurse took hold. The town of Marfa was unusual when Irma was growing up. With Sul Ross University nearby, each student was encouraged to go to college. Irma was among the ninety percent of high school graduates in Marfa who went on to college.

The same English teacher who encouraged Irma drove her to El Paso after graduation to attend nursing school. Irma's family had no car, even though her mother worked many hours a day to support them.

Irma received her diploma from the nursing school in El Paso. She married her high school sweetheart and, eager to continue her education, re-enrolled in college. The couple's first child was born while Irma was going to college. She finished her degree, earning a bachelor of science in nursing at West Texas State University in Canyon, Texas. She worked as a nurse in several hospitals in West Texas as she studied for her degree.

With her high school teacher's words still echoing in her mind, Irma went on to earn two master's degrees: one in counseling and one in nursing. She worked during this time, raising a family of three children. She gives credit to her children, who helped with household chores, but especially to her husband, who encouraged her to pursue her goals.

Irma has always taken time to participate in church and community activities. She was president of the school board at St. Mary's Catholic School in Odessa, board member of the Hospice of the Southwest, member of American Heart Association Board, and active in many other groups. Her honors are many, but two are very special. She was named to Who's Who Among American Teachers and also to the Texas Hall of Fame.

Irma has published many medical articles. Most of these are related to either nursing or psychology, the study of human behavior. She did extensive research studying the effects of depression on sleep patterns of Mexican-Americans.

Irma wants to unite her sleep research with her training as a psychiatric nurse practitioner. "People who are depressed have very poor quality of sleep," she said. "That could relate to the way people perform."

Her emphasis as a nurse practitioner is to help people, especially Mexican-Americans, with depression and other problems. She will be working with a physician to treat patients with psychological problems. Her training and extensive education will enable her to diagnose and treat people.

"I've always had a dream and envied people with knowledge. I hope to contribute my knowledge to others.

"Everything starts with a dream. Instead of asking a young person what they want to be when they grow up, I would ask them, 'What is your dream?' It's up to the person to make that dream a reality."

Vikki Carr
ENTERTAINER

Little Florencia Cardona hummed the tune while her father played the guitar. She was performing in a Christmas play at the age of four.

"I looked up to see my mother crying," she said. "I thought that I had disappointed her. Then she told me she was crying because she was proud of me."

Since then she has seldom stopped singing. Born Florencia Bisenta de Castillas Martinez Cardona in El Paso, Texas, she is now known as Vikki Carr—international star. She changed her name by taking her saint's name, Bisenta (Vikki in English), and shortening her last name, Cardona, to Carr. She has won three Grammy Awards and produced fifty-two best-selling albums, including seventeen gold albums.

Vikki spoke only Spanish when she started school, but quickly learned English. With her innate talent for music, Vikki began performing in elementary school and later sang in her high school a capella choir and school musicals. She began singing with a band while still a student. As her career advanced, Vikki toured with bands, gave concerts, and recorded albums. Vikki is a natural entertainer who charms her audience with her warm personality and lyrical voice.

Vikki Carr
—*Courtesy of M.P.I. Talent Agency*

Although American audiences were slow to appreciate her talent, Vikki received wide acclaim as she toured Australia and England. She was asked to perform for Queen Elizabeth II in London in 1967 and later had a series of sold-out concerts in Western Europe and Japan. She also entertained troops in Vietnam during the war—an experience she will never forget.

Television opened up new opportunities for Vikki. Her smiling face and musical ability soon won the admiration of many Americans. She was invited to perform in such famous resort cities as Reno, Las Vegas, and Lake Tahoe. One of her all-time hits, "It Must Be Him," was nominated for a Grammy Award in 1967. Much later, the song was featured in the movie *Moonstruck*.

She won leading roles in various musicals: *The Unsinkable Molly Brown*, *South Pacific*, and *I'm Getting My Act Together and Taking It On the Road*. She also guest-starred on the popular syndicated television program *Baywatch* as the mother of Jose Salano. In 1972 Vikki decided to release her first album in Spanish: *Vikki Carr en Español* and *Vikki Carr Hoy*. She brushed up on her native tongue, Spanish, to record these albums. She was honored in Mexico as "Visiting Entertainer of the Year." Her Spanish language albums have won gold, platinum, and diamond awards.

Her 1992 album *Cosas del Amor* won the Grammy Award as "Best Latin Pop Album." This popular hit was recorded with Mexican singer Ana Gabriel. While performing in Mexico, Vikki rediscovered mariachi music. From this discovery she teamed up with Linda Ronstadt to sing with mariachi groups in California and in Arizona.

Vikki is proud of her Hispanic heritage. Although keeping a busy schedule, she still takes time to do things for others. When she heard of Holy Cross High School in San Antonio having financial problems, she arranged for benefit concerts, giving her talent and time to raise

$250,000 for the school. To show their appreciation, the students and faculty named the library for Vikki Carr.

She also organized a Vikki Carr Scholarship Foundation to encourage Mexican-American youth to go to college. The Foundation has awarded over 200 scholarships to students who have studied at universities all over the country. Vikki had a role in selecting these students.

She has been honored by many groups, and in various ways, including "Woman of the Year" by the *Los Angeles Times,* "Singer of the Year" by The American Guild of Variety Artists, and "Hispanic Woman of the Year."

Vikki Carr's gift for expressing herself in music has touched many people. Her songs often tell a story—sad or happy. She has experienced both these emotions in her life and feels she has become stronger because of them. She is happy to have found the love of her life, Dr. Pedro DeLeon. They live in San Antonio, Texas, and Vikki is delighted to have three stepchildren and several grandchildren. "I love to be with them and even be called Grandma," she says.

Vikki does not look like a grandmother. Her honey colored hair frames a soft face and genuine smile. She has a touch of glamour about her, but she is friendly, encouraging others to know her and her feelings. She may stop during a concert and invite the audience to ask questions about her career or life. Her rapport with the audience shows her interest in people and desire to know them.

"When I go to a foreign country, and don't know the language, I communicate by smiling and making eye contact. I want to understand people and show love. Love is very important."

Her schedule is very busy as she tours with her

band all over the country. She has entertained at the White House for several presidents. In 1998 she performed at Carnegie Hall in a Public Broadcasting special to honor Judy Garland.

Vikki Carr began young and worked hard to achieve her present success. She had the good fortune to have parents who encouraged her. When asked if she would encourage young people today to enter show business, she answered honestly.

"If performing is in their hearts, then they should surely try it. They [would] never forgive themselves if they didn't. But this should not be sacrificed for an education. That comes first. An education can help them in whatever field they enter. Show business is harder today. Trends and times change so fast that it's difficult to keep up. Performers have to keep reinventing themselves to stay in the mainstream."

Vikki is versatile in interpreting many types of music from past years to today's tunes. She may sing a boisterous, rhythmic piece that shows the drama and strength of her voice. Or she may show tenderness in a love ballad as her voice reaches for the right emotion. She sometimes ends a concert with a serious, moving piece called "Por Amor" ("For Love"), giving it her own personal touch.

As she sings the words in Spanish, the audience, regardless of their language, understands the emotion behind the song. Vikki's voice and music encourage the audience to agree that "Love is universal and essential to world peace."

Hector Galan
FILMMAKER

The clock strikes four A.M.,
The vaquero's day begins,
Riding across the dusty plains,
Wide-brimmed hat over his eyes,
Riding, roping 'til dark.
He tells his story,
Guitar music softly playing.

This passage describes a scene from *Vaquero: The Forgotten Cowboy,* a film made by Hector Galan. A narrator tells the story of the early cowboys, the Mexican *vaqueros.* The narrator explains that the *vaquero's* work will soon be over, replaced by trucks and helicopters. Old *vaqueros* tell first-hand of their experiences.

This is not a movie with actors. Those in the film are real people who talk about their lives on ranches in South Texas. Hector Galan has been making films like this for over twenty years. They are called documentary films because they present factual information in an artistic way.

Many of Galan's films are shown on public television. Since they present facts and history, they are timeless. Galan is a specialist in making documentaries.

He began his television career as a teenager in San

Hector Galan —Courtesy of Hector Galan

Angelo, Texas. As cameraman for the evening news, he gained experience and a desire to make films. After moving to Lubbock, he studied filmmaking at Texas Tech. He was also local news director on the NBC affiliate. He learned how to report news and understand what appeals to the public. At that point he began directing public affairs programming on public television. One of his first ventures in national programming came in 1980 with the series *Checking It Out*.

This program had great appeal for Hispanic teenagers. The twenty-six-part series dealt with social issues, sports, and celebrities. It won an award from Action on Children's Television.

Since then Galan has produced many popular documentaries. His films entertain as well as inform the audience about important subjects. Two of his films about drugs were called *Stopping Drugs* and *The Dallas Drug War*. These told the facts and gave the consequences of taking drugs, and illustrated the efforts made to stop the practice.

Galan, deeply interested in Tejano music, produced an entertaining documentary, *Songs of the Homeland*. Freddy Fender narrates the Texas-Mexican experience with music describing each year. Old film clips flash on the screen as people tell of their experiences. The traditional accordion music is played by Mexican musicians. Trends in Tejano music continue to the rock-and-roll era, with the use of electronic instruments and *conjunto* tunes. Little Joe y La Familia provided music for the soundtrack. Later, Galan produced a tribute to Selena on the first anniversary of her death.

One of his most successful films is *Chicano: History of the Civil Rights Movement,* which was first shown in 1996 in theaters across the United States. With Henry Cisneros as narrator, the film covers the years from 1965 to 1975. It shows the people's struggle for land. It features Cesar Chavez and the farm workers' strike for decent wages. The film reveals how non-violent demonstrations can create changes that benefit the people.

Another of Galan's achievements was being selected as staff producer for the award-winning *Frontline* series on PBS from Boston. One of the films in this series was *Chasing the Basketball Dream,* which compared college athletics to education and learning.

The *American Experience* programs on public television are popular and informative. Galan's *The Hunt for Pancho Villa* in this series won several awards, including the important Spur Award for "Best Western TV Script-Documentary." This was given by the Western Writers of America.

Besides staying busy with his film company, Galan takes time to teach others the craft of making films for television. In 1998 he conducted workshops in Alaska as well as in Hawaii and Guam. He taught public affairs production in Boston for national producers. He enjoys working with high school students in the Rio Grande Valley, and for the Austin Community Public Access television station. He has held workshops at the University of Texas at Austin in the Radio-Television-Film Department.

Galan has won many awards and honors. He was named one of the 100 most influential Americans by *Hispanic Business Magazine.* In 1998 Fox 7 News in Austin selected him as Person of the Week for Outstanding Community Service. The Nosotros Golden Eagle Award was awarded to him for Outstanding Documentary.

Galan is never without new projects and ideas. A film, *Winter Texans in South Texas,* is being made. A documentary, *South Texas Land Grants,* will interest many people. *Children of the Colonias,* a look at people living in poverty conditions near the Mexican border, is another film being considered.

Hector Galan will be making important films for years to come. He has had many interesting experiences in his career but remembers one as being very speical:

"An experience I will never forget was being invited to the White House for a private screening of my film, *Chicano,* by the president of the United States."

What does he say to young people interested in film or television careers?

"Focus your energy, persevere, and with hard work, your career goals will be a reality."

Carmen Lomas Garza
ARTIST AND WRITER

"My mother Maria was the first artist I saw paint. I was about eight years old, and she was painting the *tablas* [picture cards] for *loteria* [a Mexican game similar to bingo] with pen, ink, and watercolors. I thought she was making magic," Carmen wrote in her book, *Mi Familia.*

The memory of this day stayed with her and influenced her life. Five years later, at age thirteen, she decided she wanted to be an artist. She practiced each day, drawing ordinary things—flowers, her brothers and sisters, whatever was in front of her. She is now a successful artist with paintings and *papel picado* (cut-paper art) that have been displayed in galleries and museums throughout the United States and Mexico.

Her art is based on memories from her childhood. In one painting she draws her family making *empanadas* with a sweet potato filling. Another shows the family decorating Easter eggs *(cascarones)*, or breaking a *piñata* at a birthday party. Her art shows details of a Mexican family doing typical family things. She uses reds, yellows, and other warm colors to describe true events in her life. She might paint a Saturday night dance at *El Jardin* with a *conjunto* band: accordion, guitar, and

Carmen Lomas Garza
—Courtesy of Children's Book Press

bass. The details in her paintings make her artwork special.

Carmen was born in Kingsville, Texas, near the Mexican border. She has always been proud of her heritage. Her father's family moved to Texas because of the Mexican Revolution. Her mother's family included *vaqueros* (early cowboys). Carmen's art and writing clearly show how essential her ancestry is as she communicates with pictures and words. Traditions and customs are important to her.

"Every time I paint, it serves a purpose—to bring about pride in our Mexican-American heritage," she says.

Her parents wanted all their children to go to college and pursue their individual interests. Carmen chose to study art, the subject she loves the most. She completed her art education in Texas and received a studio art degree in California. While in college, she took part in efforts to help Mexican-Americans receive equal opportunities.

She compares her painting to the aloe vera plant. Its cool liquid soothes and heals. Creating art has helped her with some of the hurts she felt as a child. Expressing herself has made her feel better about herself and her culture.

Carmen has also written and illustrated children's books. Her stories are easily understood, like the artwork that accompanies them. The books are bilingual, written in Spanish and in English, each version on opposite pages from each other. Her first book, *Family Pictures (Cuadros de Familia),* was published in 1990 and has received several honors. It won the American Library Association's Notable Award, the Texas Bluebonnet Award, and the American Library Association's Award for Latino literature.

A Piece of My Heart (Pedacito de mi Corazon) was published in 1991. *In My Family (En mi Familia)* was published in 1996. It received the American Picture Book Award as well as the Tomás Rivera Award for excellence in Latino children's literature.

Carmen now lives in San Francisco, where she works hard at creating art and writing books for children. It may take from two to nine months to complete a painting, she says. During this time she paints up to six hours a day. She sells many of her paintings and prints. Yet sometimes it is difficult for her to part with a painting because she puts so much of herself into it.

"My paintings are like my children," she says.

Although she does not have one favorite painting, she does enjoy painting some objects more than others. She likes painting houses, especially bedrooms and kitchens. And she likes to paint clothing, especially clothes her mother made for her as a child.

Carmen Lomas Garza is one of the first women of Mexican-American ancestry to be recognized nationally in the art world. Her work has been exhibited throughout the United States, Mexico, Puerto Rico, Venezuela, and Spain. She has received fellowships for study from the National Endowment for the Arts. Carmen Lomas Garza will continue to be an influential artist and individual well into the twenty-first century.

Eligio (Kika) de la Garza
UNITED STATES CONGRESSMAN

Kika de la Garza grew up in the Lower Rio Grande Valley of Texas. As a child, he picked cotton, beans, tomatoes, and peppers from nearby farms. Almost everyone in this farming community either planted or harvested vegetables and fruits, or worked in the canning plants. They supplied Texas and other states with food. Kika de la Garza never forgot these farms and farmers. Years later he would remember and try to help them when he became a United States Congressman.

Now retired, De la Garza is a friendly man who entertains politicians and other government officials in Texas and in Washington, DC. His sense of humor and reputation as a storyteller and "spinner of yarns" have made him legendary.

Growing up two miles from the Mexican border near Mercedes, Texas, his roots go back to the early 1700s in the Rio Grande Valley, over 250 years before Texas was a state. His family was known as one of the "old families." De la Garza spent much time with his grandparents and an uncle named Enrique, called Kika for short. Since Eligio tagged after his uncle, he became known as Little Kika. He is called Kika today.

De la Garza attended high school in Mission, Texas,

Eligio (Kika) de la Garza (right) with Dr. Miguel A. Nevarez, president of University of Texas, Pan American, in 1999 as he donates his congressional papers to the University.
—Courtesy of University of Texas–Pan American

and enlisted in the Navy at age seventeen during World War II. After his service he attended Edinburg Junior College and later received his law degree from St. Mary's University in San Antonio.

During the Korean War he re-entered the military, serving as an officer in the U.S. Army. During a ten-day leave, he campaigned for a spot in the Texas legislature and was elected. One of his staunch supporters in the election was Lucille Alamia. He married her a short time later, and they have three children: Jorge, Michael, and Angela.

As a state legislator, he supported educational bills for the public schools of Texas. He helped Pan American University become part of the state university system. During this time he proved himself as a self-taught master of many languages. He was often called upon to meet with leaders from foreign countries since he could speak to them in their own tongue, whether it was French, Italian, Portuguese, or another language.

After twelve years as state legislator, he ran for the U.S. Congress. He became the first Hispanic American elected from Texas' 15th District. He spent the next thirty-two years in Washington.

"Government is everybody's business, and any man who serves as representative of the people should fairly and courageously reflect the people's views," he once said.

The Democratic congressman helped improve relations between the United States and Mexico. He fought for educational opportunities for all children and made many improvements in the agricultural business.

In 1989 he said, "The farmer is a special person. The Good Lord made him that way. He was made to produce off the land, to feed God's children."

De la Garza was the first Hispanic to become chairman of the Agricultural Committee of the United States. When he took the job, he faced some of the toughest years on record for agriculture. He worked for the farmers who grow food for our country to make sure they did not go bankrupt. He became the overseer of all operations in the United States Department of Agriculture and passed bills to help the farmers when crops failed, or a drought, freeze, or other crisis occurred.

He expressed his views this way: "There is a tremendous gap between the consumer and the fellow who rides on the tractor or who is picking the fruit. I would like to be remembered as the chairman who put it all together . . . legislative programs in agriculture . . . [with] the farmers, ranchers, and consumers."

De la Garza was also involved in international affairs. He became the adviser in Congress to Europe, the Middle East, the Far East, and most countries of Latin America. He successfully met with foreign leaders, making them feel at home in the United States. He was and is still a firm believer in education, insisting that "Education is the key."

He recalls one of his most memorable experiences in his long career in Washington. He introduced his first bill to help farmers when he was chairman of the Agriculture Committee. The bill seemed doomed to failure, but at the last minute, it passed by two votes, 205-203. At the end, the Congress stood up and applauded Kika de la Garza for a full five minutes.

He was named "Mr. South Texas" on February 19, 1989, at a birthday celebration of George Washington, sometimes called the "Father of our Country." Jim Wright, then Speaker of the House of Representatives, said, "Kika, the wonderful thing is that you are a builder of bridges, not walls."

Indeed, Kika de la Garza has been called the "ambassador" of agriculture and the "architect" of better understanding between the United States, Mexico, and Central America. Other countries have honored him for his international accomplishments. Mexico gave him their highest award, the Aztec Eagle Award. Israel presented him with a Lifetime Achievement Award. He also received an honorary degree from Hanyang University in Korea.

De la Garza announced in 1995 that he would not seek re-election to Congress. While still in office he worked to streamline services such as Medicaid, health, and education, as well as programs for the elderly and poor. He also wanted very much to balance the country's budget. He has resumed law practice in McAllen, Texas, and is enjoying his family, which includes seven grandchildren.

"There are many things I want to do while I'm in good health—young enough," he said as he left his long career in government for a slower, quieter life. "One of these things is to write the real history of Texas. I want to include Hispanics; the Mexican Americans who helped make this state what it is today."

Tish Hinojosa
MUSICIAN AND FOLKSINGER

Tish Hinojosa strums her guitar, singing in her clear, lyrical voice. She smiles often, enjoying performing as much as the audience enjoys her singing. Her dark hair trails her shoulders as she charms her audience in a quiet, gracious way. She has been an entertainer for half of her life, ever since she was a teenager in San Antonio. She has performed in the United States, Europe, and Mexico. Her albums have been heard by people everywhere.

Tish has loved music since she was a small child. She remembers going to her backyard near the San Antonio River and singing the songs she heard on the radio and television. Her parents never expected her to be a well-known performer since she was a shy child who stayed at home much of the time.

"There was always music in the house," she recalls. "My mother listened to Mexican radio in the kitchen, and she loved the finer, romantic side of Mexican culture. My dad was a mechanic, and he loved the fun accordion music and *conjunto* tunes."

Tish was born with musical talent and taught herself to play guitar on a borrowed instrument. The youngest in a family of thirteen children, Tish heard only

Tish Hinojosa
—Photo by Wyatt McSpadden

Spanish from her parents. She did not learn English as a young child since she was ill much of the time and stayed at home with her mother. She remembers starting first grade without knowing any English. She felt as if she was in a foreign country—out of place and insecure.

Because of this early experience, she now works to promote bilingual education for the National Latino Children's Agenda. She hopes to spare other children the pain and isolation she felt as a young girl. She doesn't want today's children to feel that their language is being taken from them.

Tish grew up in a strict Catholic family, and attended Providence High School for Girls in San Antonio. She is grateful for the discipline and education she received at home and at school. These influences helped her develop strong values and good habits.

She began her career as singer and guitarist when she was a teenager in San Antonio. Because her mother was strict, she insisted that Tish's older sister and brother-in-law chaperon her. She always felt she was part of two cultures: Mexican and American.

"When my family would go to Mexico," she recalls, "we'd be called *Las Americanas;* here in the states, we'd be called Mexicans."

That is probably the reason her singing and songwriting career shows both these cultures. While still a teenager, she sang American folk songs in clubs, then performed Spanish ballads on the River Walk.

"My ancestry is Mexican, but it's not my whole picture. I'm just as American. We had turkey for Thanksgiving, maybe a bowl of salsa on the table."

Tish is described as a folk singer who combines the best of both these worlds. She often begins a song in English, then changes to Spanish for the next verse. Critics feel she is able to achieve an unusual blend without disrupting the song. Since music is called the international language, people can listen and appreciate both languages even if they only speak one of them.

After performing for several years, she moved to northern New Mexico and lived near a songwriter's colony. This experience helped develop her talent for composing music. The Southwestern influence also made her feel close to her Hispanic roots. The first two songs that she wrote won top prizes at the Kerrville Folk Festival.

She spent some time in Nashville but decided to return to Texas to compose and perform the kind of music she loved: a blend of Hispanic and American folk music. She grew up on the west side of San Antonio, where many people from Mexico came to live. One of her albums called *Homeland* tells the stories of immigrants in a strange land. Her song, "West Side," is the story of her mother and father who struggled to raise their thirteen children.

Tish often introduces her songs, telling the background, and why she wrote them. She communicates with her audience well, using just the right words to describe her feelings, the circumstances, and how the idea caught her interest.

One of her songs, "Chanate, the Vaquero," is a lively song about a Mexican cowboy. In her album *Las Fronterias,* she sings about frontier women who fought for people's rights along with the men in the Mexican Revolution of 1910.

Family life is important to Tish. Not only is she grateful to her parents for their love and sacrifices, but she cherishes the extended family. She remembers her grandmother with love and affection. Tish visited her as a small child and can still smell the kerosene lamps in her grandmother's small apartment in Mexico; there was no electricity. At times her sisters have wondered why Tish has such fond memories. "She was not very grandmotherly," she says with a smile. "She did not like housekeeping at all. What she liked to do was drink coffee and tell stories. I loved her and her stories."

Tish wrote a song about this grandmother. When she sings it, she smiles and seems to remember the days when she visited her grandmother and did not want to leave. It is called *"Siempre Abuelita"* (Always Grandma), and part of it goes like this:

> *Always, always, Grandma,*
> *All my life I'll be*
> *Full of love I won't forget,*
> *That you have given me.*

One of her dreams came true in 1996, when she was invited to sing and play in front of the White House in a program honoring Hispanic leaders. Soon after this, she toured throughout the United States. She has performed at many benefit concerts, including the United Farm Workers and Habitat for Humanity. One of her favorite things to do is to play and sing at ceremonies when new immigrants become citizens.

Tish is very fond of children and has two of her own. Her children have inspired her to write special songs. She made an album called *Cada Niño* (Each Child), which is mainly for children.

She wrote the words to "Nina Violina" (Robert Skiles wrote the music), to teach her children Spanish. She and her children wrote verses about everyday events and kept them in a notebook with pictures so they could remember the words. When her daughter, Nina, was seven, she played the violin well enough to accompany her mother and teacher on the recording. The following is one verse from the song:

> *We are arising early this morning*
> *Apple bread waiting, breakfast is calling.*

Love in a smile and a heart beating,
What a good way each day beginning.

This bilingual song has received many awards, including the Parent's Choice Gold Award and one from the National Association for Parenting.

Her Texas roots are very important to her. Not long ago she recorded an album, *Dreaming from the Labyrinth*. She chose the old Ursuline Convent chapel in San Antonio for the setting. She wanted the album, composed of ten songs (five in English and five in Spanish) to have a spiritual feeling. Many of her songs are inspired by literature, stories, and poems. She visits used book stores and often finds the perfect story that inspires a song. Although she enjoys performing, songwriting is her real love. A new song she has written is about Americo Paredes, a famous folklorist. He has been a mentor to Tish and taught her Mexican folklore.

Tish lives in Austin with her children and husband, Craig Barker, an attorney. She enjoys visiting schools and telling the students about her Hispanic heritage and the songs she writes. She wants them to know that the songs came from her Mexican-American heritage.

"Here in America we all come from different cultural backgrounds. This is a wonderful thing that we should treasure and respect in each other. I am proud of being American and very proud of my Mexican-American heritage," she told a group of students recently.

"There is a saying in Spanish that my mother used when I was growing up, *Querer es poder*. This means to want is to do. This worked for Mom, and it works for me.

"I'm a working Mom with two kids. I embrace people. They embrace me."

Luis Jiménez
SCULPTOR

Luis Jiménez's sculptures shine in the sunlight. The figures, some larger than life, attract passersby with their reds, yellows, blues, and other bright colors. The sculptures speak to those who listen, with a message or a story.

His *Vaquero,* a Mexican cowboy riding a bronco, imparts action and energy. The *Sodbuster* shows a hardworking farmer pushing a plow with a team of oxen, a scene that pays tribute to our past. Luis Jiménez reminds us of our history and who we are.

It is not by accident that many of his sculptures appear outdoors or in large areas where many people can see them. He believes that art should be made public, available to everyone, not just those who visit museums and galleries.

You will find his sculptures in parks, airports, school campuses, and wherever people gather. He does not use material such as bronze or marble, as many sculptors before him did. Instead, he works with fiberglass to create his unique art forms. He can cast a mold and make five or six sculptures from that mold. This way he can distribute his work in more areas and take his art to the public.

The feel of fiberglass is not new to Jiménez. He grew up in El Paso, watching and helping in his father's sign

Luis Jiménez
—Photo courtesy of Mieko Mahi

shop. His father was a creative businessman whose signs and billboards caught the attention of customers. Many of them were large, some with neon lights. He also molded polar bears and other animals used in advertising. As a boy, Luis, Jr., hung around his dad's shop and learned about making models from fiberglass.

Luis was interested in art and showed talent as a boy. He won his first art contest when he was in first grade. He continued his art projects in school and won the admiration of teachers, especially his junior high art teacher. He took his first trip to Mexico City when he was six, an experience he never forgot. He went to Mexico many times as an adult to see the pyramids and artwork made by the Olmec and Mayans.

Jiménez attended the University of Texas at Austin, where he studied art and architecture. On long visits to Mexico he studied such great artists as Orozco, Siquieros, and Rivera.

Like many artists he felt that he needed to go to New York City after college and be a part of the art world there. He worked for another sculptor before striking out on his own, creating drawings, paintings, and sculptures. He succeeded in having his work on exhibit and was selling enough to support himself. Yet he was not satisfied. He felt the need to touch more people with his art. His belief that art should be made public and reach a wider audience caused him to leave the city. "I wanted to reach a broader audience, and I was really interested in the concept of public art."

There were few examples of modern art in public places at that time, especially sculpture. He got the opportunity to try out his ideas in New Mexico.

In 1972 he moved to Roswell, New Mexico, an area closer to his Western roots, its culture, and influences. As artist-in-residence, he painted a series of murals for the city. This was the first time his dream of creating art for all people began to materialize. He called the murals "Progress Pieces," a tribute to the murals of the Work Projects Administration during the Depression.

During this time he saw an old schoolhouse in Hondo, New Mexico. He bought it, then remodeled it with a studio downstairs and living area upstairs. Luis, his wife, and three children still live there. He works in his studio except for each spring when he teaches at the University of Houston.

Luis Jiménez likes for people to discuss his art and express their feelings about it. Art should be interactive and suggest ideas, he believes. *Border Crossing,* a favorite sculpture of his, shows a Mexican father carrying his wife and baby across the river. He dedicated it to his parents who emigrated from Mexico in the 1920s. This sculpture expresses a sense of family.

Jiménez's work suggests a new way of looking at the American West; i.e., a more modern approach. They show figures in action, like the bold *Vaquero* and real-life *Fiesta Dancers.* His sculptures can be found in cities from San Diego to Washington, DC. The National Museum of American Art in Washington, the Metropolitan Museum of Art, and the Museum of Modern Art in New York City own Jiménez's sculptures.

In 1998 his glossy statues, *Mesteño* and *Howl,* were exhibited at the ACA Museum in New York City with Jiménez present. Soon the thirty-two-foot-tall *Mustang* will be on view at the new Denver International Airport.

Two other sculptures can be seen at the University of Texas at San Antonio, three at El Paso, and one in Dallas. The *Vaquero,* or Mexican cowboy, is enjoyed by those who visit Moody Park in Houston. Strake Jesuit High School in Houston has five sculptures which help students understand and appreciate art.

Jiménez has achieved his goal of bringing art to the public. He has combined his own experience growing up in an immigrant neighborhood of El Paso with the study of great Mexican artists in Mexico City. His sculptures may be seen in many museums as well as in public places throughout the United States.

Jiménez returned to his alma mater in October of 1998 to receive the Distinguished Alumnus Award, the highest award the alumni association gives. This makes him the first visual artist to be honored in the history of the award.

Linda Sagarnaga Magill
PHYSICIAN

Linda Magill always wanted to be a doctor. Getting into medical school was difficult enough, especially for a Hispanic woman. But having to juggle motherhood while studying to be a doctor made it more difficult. She had been taught that mothers stayed home with their children. She did that when her first child, a son, was born. But when a baby girl arrived in the middle of her medical training, she could not quit school. She and her husband, Patrick Magill, worked it out. Since she was on duty as a resident every third night, her husband became Mr. Mom. He was the parent their baby cried for in the middle of the night. It hurt sometimes to give up this time of her daughter's life, but the situation was only temporary.

"My husband was very supportive. He believed in me and wanted me to realize my dream of becoming a doctor."

In fact, they were supportive of each other. They had married while they were quite young and before either of them had any college training. But they each had the goal of finishing their education, and they helped each other. They took turns going to school while the other worked. It took Linda Magill seven years to

Linda Sagarnaga Magill
—Courtesy of Linda Magill

graduate from college since she worked part-time. She was the first on her mother's side of the family to get a bachelor's degree. She was twenty-nine by the time she enrolled at the University of Texas Medical School in Houston. She had worked in the school's research department before she was admitted as a medical student.

Linda's favorite subject in school was science. She had this interest as a very young child growing up in Houston. "My cousin teased me because I wasn't afraid to pick up a dead animal or an insect," she said.

Her immediate family consisted of her parents and one brother. Her extended family, which included grandparents, aunts, uncles, and many cousins, was very close. She remembers that as a child she stayed with family members when her mother had to work.

She also remembers that during these years her parents were involved in different Hispanic organizations in Houston. She often helped her mother stuff envelopes in preparation for a fund-raising benefit for such organizations as the Institute of Hispanic Culture. She and her mother, Minerva Sagarnaga, have worked for the Houston Hispanic Forum for almost fifteen years. Volunteering for worthy causes is part of their lives.

The Houston Hispanic Forum sponsors an annual career and education day for students. Young people attend an all-day session listening to speeches from people representative of many vocations. They learn about different types of careers and how to qualify for them. Dr. Magill knows well that it is important for a student to have a helping hand as he/she tries to choose a career.

"I feel I have been helping someone all along the way," she said. "You feel a part of the community and it makes you a better person. There is always someone who needs direction."

She remembers a woman doctor from Mexico who inspired her. The successful physician was assertive, confident, and not afraid to speak her mind when the occasion demanded it. Linda Magill learned a few lessons from this doctor since she was quiet and shy. She learned how to communicate and assert herself in a hospital where most of the doctors are male.

One of Dr. Magill's most rewarding yet difficult experiences occurred when she was doing her residency. This is the time in a doctor's career when he or she must work in all areas of the hospital to understand all kinds of medical situations.

"I was on call every third night," she said. "One night I was the senior physician, totally in charge in the intensive care unit. I was responsible for patients with kidney, lung, and heart transplants. I was also in charge of donor organs, [from] those who die suddenly and want to donate an organ to a living person. I had to make all the decisions. Many lives were at stake, and I was in charge. That was a tough but very rewarding experience."

Dr. Linda Magill rose to the occasion and made the right decisions. Since that time she has gained confidence in her ability to deal with crises and very sick people. She has proven she has the stamina and skill in her role as anesthesiologist, a doctor who helps keep patients from having pain during operations and other medical procedures. She has to know exactly what kind of medicine and how much to give each patient.

Dr. Linda Magill speaks of her career as a doctor with love and dedication. She feels fortunate to be a doctor. "It is a rare opportunity to make a living doing what you want to do. I am one of those blessed people."

Although her career is often stressful, she has no regrets about choosing the medical profession. She feels she was meant to be a doctor, and her work has not interfered with her personal life.

"I'm a better mother because I have a meaningful occupation."

Dr. Linda Sagarnaga Magill has combined a career with the role of wife and mother, and enjoys a rich, rewarding life. She has not forgotten her Mexican-American heritage and uses her talents both as a doctor and volunteer.

Pat Mora
WRITER, TEACHER

When Pat Mora visits her hometown of El Paso, Texas, dozens of memories flash into her mind. Growing up in a border town in a bilingual extended family has influenced her life and her writing. No matter where she is, this region of the Southwest remains part of her. She has written over twenty books that illustrate her knowledge and love for the area as well as the affection and loyalty she has for her family, past and present. Some of these books have won outstanding awards.

Her father crossed the nearby Rio Grande with his parents when he was three years old. He was selling newspapers by the time he was seven, giving what he earned to his mother to help the family.

Both parents were good role models to their children but very different. Her father was quiet and hardworking, while her mother liked to participate in activities and was praised for her ability to speak. Pat benefited from both of these role models. She also felt nurtured by a large extended family.

Family history and heritage are often the subjects of Mora's poetry, essays, and stories. One of her favorite people is her Aunt Ignacia, who read to Pat and her sisters when they were children. This aunt was also a good

Pat Mora —Photo by Cynthia Farah

storyteller, who told her nieces stories of growing up in Mexico and then coming to the United States. One of Pat's picture books, *A Birthday Basket for Tia,* was inspired by this special aunt.

Many other children's books followed this one, including *Tomás and the Library Lady,* a story about the writer Tomás Rivera. The son of migrant workers, he picked fruits and vegetables along with his family. He later became a writer and college president. The library lady in the story introduced him to the world of books and learning, which changed his life. This book was chosen a Texas Bluebonnet book in 1999.

This Big Sky is a book of poems that tells in musical language about the Chihuahua Desert and the Southwest. Pat Mora describes the people, the animals, and the landscape with vivid images. The reader can envision the coyote, the raccoon, the land, and its people. This book was given a special award by the Book Publishers of Texas.

"The sky is big enough for all my dreams," she says.

"My friends who write for adults don't know what they're missing. In many ways children's books are a particular sense of joy to me," she told a reporter from the *Houston Chronicle* (May 30, 1999).

Pat has received praise for her adult books, as well. She has published books of poems for older readers, such as *Chants, Aunt Carmen's Book of Practical Saints,* and her autobiography, *House of Houses.* This book describes Pat's background and shows her insight and love for family and the Southwest.

"As the rose is the flower of flowers, this is the house of houses, *'nuestra casa de casa,'*" she says about her childhood home in El Paso. In her autobiography she describes the setting of the home near the Rio Grande with its piñon trees, courtyard, yuccas, and giant mesquite tree that towers over the children's swing.

The poetic writing makes memories come alive as Pat speaks to her past ancestors as well as her living family members. Voices speak from the rooms of the house, each telling a unique story, and revealing a distinct personality. There is her tall, quiet father, and her talkative, outgoing mother, as well as grandparents, aunts, and uncles. Pat weaves the family history together like a fine woolen shawl. Her relatives speak from her imagination in twelve different chapters, beginning with January and ending with December.

"I love words and their power to move us, to entertain us, to make us laugh, to comfort us," she said.

Growing up in a bilingual home was a blessing for Pat, who speaks and writes in Spanish and English. Several of her children's books are bilingual, in which the story appears in both languages in the same book. As a child, the Spanish she spoke to her aunts and grandmother was not the language she wanted her childhood friends to hear. Today she is proud of being able to speak the language of her family. She feels she is a part of two worlds, both in language and in culture. She spends most of her time in Cincinnati, Ohio, but still feels a part of the Southwest. She especially likes the months she spends teaching at the University of New Mexico.

Pat graduated from the Loretto Academy in El Paso. This school, its chapel and surroundings still have a special meaning to her. It was in this school that she received an excellent education and learned the importance of treating everyone with respect.

After high school, she attended and graduated from the University of Texas at El Paso, then taught high school English for several years. She also married and had three children, all of whom are now adults. After earning her master's degree in English, she became an instructor at the University of Texas at El Paso, later becoming an administrator at the university and museum director.

Pat has the ability to speak well in public, as her mother did before her. This talent contributed to her success as host of a radio show in El Paso, called "Voices: The Mexican American Perspective." She also uses this skill in the classroom.

She received the Kellogg Fellowship, which enabled her to travel to other countries and study their cultures. This experience was very helpful when she returned to teach others how to preserve their individual cultures. She sincerely believes that family and cultural traditions must be appreciated and maintained so they can endure. Pat reminds us that our own homes and families offer a wealth of experiences that enrich our lives. She urges young people to listen to the stories their elders tell even if they've heard them before. These stories become family history, and unless they're recorded and passed down to others, they will be lost. One way young people can preserve family history is by tape-recording the stories their relatives relate about the past. This is sometimes called oral history.

This practice of listening to others helped Pat write *House of Houses,* her autobiography. She talked to many family members as she planned her book, hearing both good and bad stories. The book is rich in the history and traditions of the Mora family.

She is concerned that more Hispanic people are not writing and contributing to American literature. She wants to hear voices and stories that express the concerns and ideas of Latinos, especially from the southwestern United States, whether this is poetry, fiction or non-fiction.

On a visit to her former elementary school in El Paso, she spoke to young children about writing. "In order to write, you must read," she told them.

Although Pat has been a teacher, speaker, and administrator, she is now deeply involved with writing. She and her husband, an archeologist, Vern Scarborough, spend part of their time in Ohio and part in New Mexico, where she often teaches.

Dan Morales
ATTORNEY GENERAL OF TEXAS

"The battle with Big Tobacco is over and the citizens of Texas are the winners. This victory presents our leaders with an unprecedented opportunity to improve our state's commitment to public health," said Dan Morales at the end of a major lawsuit with tobacco companies.

As attorney general of Texas, Dan Morales's concern for others became the reason he fought the tobacco industry in Texas. He knew tobacco was harmful to people, especially children, and fought to make tobacco companies responsible for the illnesses and deaths of people who smoked. He also wanted to keep them from advertising in public places and making smoking look like a popular thing for people to do.

Dan and his two brothers were born in San Antonio to Henry and Felicia Morales. His mother taught her three sons very early that tobacco was harmful to the body. When asked if he ever smoked, Dan Morales replied, "No kinds of cigarettes."

He remembers going to parties while attending Holmes High School in San Antonio. Sometimes alcohol and drugs were consumed, but Dan never thought "they were any big deal." This was not something he wanted

Dan Morales —Courtesy of Dan Morales

to be involved in. Dan was not perfect, though. He loved fast cars and worked every afternoon at a grocery store stocking shelves in order to buy a Pontiac Trans Am. He was proud of his car but made the mistake of speeding. He was arrested and placed in jail one night. His parents had to come for him on their way to church on Sunday morning. Embarrassed and ashamed, Dan learned his lesson the hard way. He never forgot this experience.

As a young person he enjoyed putting things together, such as model airplanes. He also played the violin well. Later, he proved himself a good tennis player. He was an average student in high school and was encouraged by his parents to go to college.

As a student at Trinity University in San Antonio, he became motivated and began to set goals for himself. He disciplined himself to study and work hard. Interested in law and government, he chose political science as his major field of study.

After graduation, he enrolled in Harvard Law School and received his degree in 1981. This won him an excellent job at a major law firm in Houston. He had a good salary, a secretary, and was on his way to becoming a well-to-do attorney, but he was not satisfied with his life. He wanted more personal satisfaction in his work. He thought a job in government would be more rewarding. He became assistant district attorney for Bexar County, taking a $15,000 cut in pay. As the assistant district attorney, he prosecuted criminals in drug-related cases.

On his summer vacation in 1983, Dan Morales traveled to the Yucatan in Mexico to help people build a church in a small village. He believes strongly that each of us has a responsibility to help others, especially those who are needy. This belief has influenced his career as public servant, both as a legislator and attorney general.

Still interested in government and public service, Morales ran for the state legislature in 1985. He wanted to represent the people of Texas, all people—all races, and all classes. To tell his story to the public, Morales knocked on hundreds of doors in San Antonio neighborhoods. His hard work and determination led to his election to the legislature when he was twenty-eight years old.

Morales spent six years working in the state legislature. He was chairman of the House Criminal Jurisprudence Committee and a member of the Ways and Means Committee. Among the crime-related bills he worked on were the Family Violence Protection Act to protect victims of crimes. He also worked to expand prisons and promoted a bill to help public education.

After six years as state representative, Morales became a candidate for the important office of attorney general of Texas. Again, he wanted to represent all the people in the state fairly. He gave the office of attorney general a different style. Morales is the first Hispanic to be elected to a state executive office.

Usually the attorney general of Texas handled civil, or non-criminal, cases. Morales began to focus on criminal justice and law enforcement reform. A slightly-built man who wears glasses, he has been compared to the Clark Kent and Superman combination. When it was necessary to take a stand or enforce an important law, Morales became "Superman" of the State Capitol.

He became concerned with the living conditions of the *colonias,* the communities on the Texas-Mexico border. Many of these poor people had no electricity, running water, or sewage connections. Morales held meetings to try to bring services to these individuals.

He has gone after "bad guys" who cheat the elderly, the poor, and the young. He fought illegal practices at hospitals and reformed nursing homes where patients did not receive good treatment. He was able to collect $1.5 million in child support payments for the children of Texas. He does not mind getting tough with those who try to break the law or abuse others.

Morales became well-known as he tackled the tobacco companies. At this point, tobacco companies had never lost a lawsuit because of their products. Morales was determined they would be responsible for their part in injuring people's health. He engaged both state and private attorneys to prove this. Most people doubted the state had a chance of winning the lawsuit.

Morales was not discouraged. "It is the right thing to do," he told citizens. And he never relented in his efforts to win the lawsuit for the people of Texas. He did not care if the issue was unpopular; he was determined to win.

"The tobacco industry has been successful in planning, implementing, and executing the largest and most destructive campaign of misinformation in U.S. business history," he said.

Skillful lawyers worked with state attorneys to prove that the tobacco companies were guilty of damaging the health of many people and causing deaths. Morales also wanted to prevent the companies from advertising in ways that influenced young people to smoke.

The state of Texas won the lawsuit. The tobacco companies will pay the state and public health agencies about $17 billion over the next twenty-five years. Each county will receive its share, based on its population. This money is to reimburse them for the treatment of tobacco-related illnesses. This large amount of money will bring better health care to citizens for many years.

Besides receiving the money, the state of Texas can now prevent tobacco companies from advertising in buses, taxis, trains, and airplanes. They must also remove all their billboards that advertise cigarettes.

Morales and his lawyers are responsible for this strong stand against tobacco.

With such a record, it seems that Morales could be assured of another term as attorney general of Texas. In 1998 he announced, however, that he would not seek reelection to the office. He married Christine Glenn, a mother of two young children, in 1997 at a small wedding at his parents' home. He now feels he wants to give more time to his new family, and will retire from public life.

Guadalupe Quintanilla
WRITER AND EDUCATOR

Guadalupe Quintanilla was labeled retarded and was not allowed to go to school or speak Spanish. Guadalupe Quintanilla is now a professor, writer, and motivational speaker with a doctorate in education.

How could a child be sentenced to a life without education? How did she overcome this barrier, this mistake?

Lupe, as her friends call her, was born in Mexico, and went to live with her grandparents as a very young child when her parents separated. She was loved very much by her grandparents, and became the center of their lives.

One day she asked her grandmother in Spanish, the only language she knew, "Nana, why am I so small?"

"Because fine things come in small packages," her grandmother replied.

Lupe's grandfather worked for the government and was gone much of the time. Her grandmother, Guadalupe Campos, ran a grocery store, bakery, and popsicle factory. Lupe stayed close to her grandmother and helped her, even as a small child. They lived in a two-story house above the grocery store. Early each morning Lupe smelled the fresh bread baking downstairs and heard her grandmother talking to the baker.

Once while playing, Lupe fell in a tub of eggs. Her

Guadalupe Quintanilla
—Courtesy of Guadalupe Quintanilla

grandmother rushed to her, worried that she was hurt. Lupe was not hurt, but it took a lot of effort to wash the sticky egg shells from her hair.

Nana taught her to read. The older woman would read the story to her, then stop before the story ended. "Tomorrow we'll finish the story," she'd say.

"Oh, please Nana, finish now," Lupe begged.

Lupe learned to read in Spanish by looking at the words and hearing her grandmother speak them. The love of reading has remained with her all her life.

"Education is the only thing I can give you," her grandmother told her.

Later, her grandparents moved to San Luis Pedro to be near their oldest son, a doctor. But there was no school for Lupe to attend. She kept reading, though, and even taught neighborhood boys and girls to read and do math.

Her grandparents moved again, this time to Matamoros, where Lupe could go to school. She made good grades and enjoyed learning. Then her grandparents moved to a farm, far away from a school. Lupe spent much of her time reading to her grandfather, who was losing his eyesight. She read books by famous Spanish writers. Finally, Lupe moved to the United States to live with her father and stepmother. She was sad to leave her grandparents but happy to go to school.

To enter school in the town of Brownsville, Lupe had to take an IQ test. Since it was written in English and Lupe knew only Spanish, she did very poorly. She was thirteen, but the principal placed her in the first grade with the younger children. Lupe was ashamed and discouraged. One day she spoke to a workman at school in Spanish and was punished. Frustrated and feeling helpless, Lupe quit school.

"They said I was retarded and couldn't learn. And to make matters worse, I believed them."

Lupe did housework for a few years, then married

Cayetano Quintanilla. At age twenty-two, Lupe had three children: Victor, Mario, and Martha. Later, when her children were in school, they too had trouble learning. They were placed in the "yellow bird" group for slow learners.

"To me they were the brightest children in the world," she said.

The school principal told her they were placed in the slow group because they did not know English. Lupe was determined to learn English and help her children learn it. She applied at several programs that taught English, but was turned down. One said she had to have a high school diploma first. Yet the public high school would not admit her.

She went to a junior college for help and convinced the school to allow her to study. She was accepted on condition that she pass the classes in English, math, and speech. Fellow students helped and tutored her. She made the dean's list that semester and each one that followed.

Lupe wanted to go on with her education after junior college and drove 140 miles each day to Pan American University in Edinburg, Texas. After three years she graduated with honors. And the best part, according to her, was seeing her children begin to do well in school.

She was in Houston visiting her parents when she decided she wanted to go to the University of Houston. She and her children moved to Houston, but her husband chose to remain in Brownsville. It was tough living in a cramped apartment with three children, but Lupe was determined to earn a master of arts degree. The University of Houston hired her to teach, and she became the first director of the Mexican-American studies program there. She also started a bilingual program so that others could study and learn English. In 1971 Lupe received the doctor of education degree.

"When someone called my house and asked for Dr. Quintanilla, I had to ask them, 'which one.' You see, all my children have doctor's degrees. One is a medical doctor, and two are lawyers."

She has taught Mexican literature and classes in Hispanic Women Writers at the University of Houston. She is now writing books about these subjects. She was elected to the Hispanic Hall of Fame and the Hispanic Women's Hall of Fame.

One program close to her heart is teaching police officers "street Spanish." It is difficult for those who speak only English to communicate with others who do not understand English. Many mistakes can be made. But Lupe is trying to help the Houston Police Department in preventing miscommunications. She is studying Vietnamese as well so that she can teach it to Houston police officers. Teaching paramedics who must deal with very ill and seriously injured people is also part of her work.

"I love to teach. I love students," she says. "People must try to understand the language and culture of others."

Manuals she has written are now used by police, paramedics, businessmen, and the FBI Academy. Dr. Quintanilla is also in demand as a motivational speaker. She travels all over the United States speaking to groups, assuring them that they too can succeed. She knows well how discouraged she was at one point in her life. But she had the determination to keep on trying. With her warmth and friendliness, she gives others confidence and hope.

She also strongly encourages students to stay in school. She believes that it is important for them to know both English and their native language. It is good to speak two languages.

She once told a group, "You want, you plan, you persist—you have the character to succeed, the ability to think, and to make things happen."

Dr. Guadalupe Quintanilla has done all these things and believes everyone can.

Hilda Tagle
UNITED STATES FEDERAL JUDGE

When Hilda Tagle was fifteen, her mother insisted she go to beauty school and learn to be a beautician. She would always have a skill and a means to support herself, her mother believed. Both her parents had been migrant workers when they were younger and knew the hardships that went with that kind of life. The young Hilda did as her mother asked, and became a beautician at age sixteen.

As a child Hilda always had her nose in a book. She loved reading and sometimes neglected her home duties to finish a book. One of her favorites, *Heidi,* stirred her imagination as she dreamed of that faraway land, Switzerland. Reading was a skill that would enable Hilda to pursue a higher education. This would eventually lead her to become a lawyer and judge.

After graduating from Robstown High School, she worked for a time in Lola's Beauty Shop. But Hilda had dreams and the ambition for a different type of life. She saved her money and attended Del Mar College, a two-year school in Corpus Christi. Wanting a university degree, she transferred to East Texas State University, working her way through school.

With her love for books and learning, she then de-

Hilda Tagle —Courtesy of Hilda Tagle

cided to go to graduate school at North Texas University, and earn a master's degree in library science. With this training, she became a librarian at Strake Jesuit Catholic High School in Houston.

During her studies at North Texas State University, she became acquainted with books about law. *Someday I'd like to study law*, she told herself. After four years as librarian, she applied at the University of Texas Law School and earned her law degree in 1977. A short time later she was hired as assistant city attorney in Corpus Christi. She was one out of only five female lawyers in the city at that time. Today, of course, this has changed and more women are entering law as well as politics. Hilda Tagle describes the change this way:

"Women are not only knocking on doors to get jobs, they are knocking *down* doors."

What she is saying is that women can assert themselves and prove to themselves and to others that they are capable of entering every profession. Hilda became interested in entering politics and holding an elective office after her experience as a city attorney. She became a prosecutor in the district attorney's office in Corpus Christi. It was her job to prove a criminal guilty of his/her crime.

She also opened a private law practice, and taught at Del Mar College before making the decision to enter public life. In 1994 she ran for judge in the 148th District of Texas. She was competing with an older judge for the position. She defeated the more experienced judge, and presided over the district until her recent appointment as federal judge.

Becoming a federal judge was a dream Hilda Tagle had, but she wondered if it would really happen. This high appointment to the judge's chambers would be a long way from her humble beginnings on poverty stricken Jefferson Street in Robstown. Hilda Tagle showed the same stubborn determination pursuing her dream as she had while earning several college degrees while working.

In 1995 President Clinton nominated Tagle for federal judge. In 1998 the United States Senate approved the nomination. She is the first woman of Hispanic heritage in Texas to reach this high position. She now presides in a national court of law, the Southern District of Texas in Brownsville.

Since only about fifteen percent of federal judges are women and even fewer are Hispanic, Hilda Tagle has achieved a significant goal. Many feel she is an important role model for women since she has proved that many careers are open to women, not just a few. Hilda Tagle believes that opportunities are there for women who are willing to get an education and take some chances. She has done both these things.

Probably because of her busy political life, she is not married. But she has raised her nephew, Santiago. When her appointment as federal judge was announced, her hometown of Robstown rejoiced. A parade was held in Judge Tagle's honor. She is a local hero who has succeeded in a big way.

Judge Tagle enjoys life although she works long hours and has much responsibility. When she relaxes, she likes to dance to Spanish music and cook. She also enjoys her many friends.

She gives credit to many people who have helped her career, especially her parents, who gave her love and support. "I wish they were here to see me," she told a reporter. "They gave me a solid foundation and every child needs to feel cherished. Feeling cherished as a child gave me confidence and self-esteem."

Frank Tejeda
UNITED STATES CONGRESSMAN

As a teenager, Frank Tejeda was called *"pachuco,"* meaning "tough"—a kid who ran with a gang and often got in trouble. His quick temper frequently led him to fighting in the neighborhood and at school. In high school his fighting caused him to be expelled. At this stage of his life, nobody expected him to achieve much.

He grew up in south San Antonio. He was a skinny boy who helped his family with expenses by mowing lawns, cleaning houses, and washing windows. Sometimes he shined shoes in cafés on Flores Street because his family needed the money.

At seventeen he left his troubled neighborhood life, joined the Marine Corps, and was sent to boot camp, which is known for its strict rules and discipline. Indeed, the loud commands of his sergeant led Tejeda into a different style of life. He began to control himself and develop ambition. The Marine Corps provided the challenge that Tejeda needed to make something of himself. He worked hard and was promoted to corporal, becoming the youngest corporal in the Marine Corps. Later, he became the youngest sergeant in the Corps.

Like many others, he was sent to Vietnam, where he proved himself a hero. He led his squad in an attack on

Frank Tejeda
—Courtesy of Texas Historical Commission

a Viet Cong sniper near Da Nang. He had to charge into battle across some seventy-five yards of open space with the enemy nearby. His squad won the skirmish and took two prisoners. Sergeant Tejeda was awarded the Bronze Star for his courage.

Only a month before he was to return to the United States, Sergeant Tejeda was wounded in action. Back in the U.S., he went to the Marine Reserve officers candidate school at Camp Quantico, Virginia. He broke all records for academic and athletic achievement. He earned a grade point average of 99.6.

Tejeda, with boyish good looks, enrolled in St. Mary's University. After graduation, he earned a law degree from the University of California. Intelligent and ambitious, he went on to earn a master's degree in public administration from the Kennedy School of Government at Harvard University. Later he received a master of law degree from Yale University.

Tejeda became an attorney in San Antonio but was considering entering politics. He wanted to help the people in San Antonio and be a spokesman for them. In 1976 he ran for the Texas legislature. He wanted to represent the old neighborhood where he grew up.

"I'd see the streets that never got repaired, the poor drainage. I'd see other people get things done because they had influence. I got involved because it was the only way I felt, to get things done," he said in 1977 as a state representative. (*San Antonio Light,* April 1, 1997)

In politics, he was also known as *"pachuco,"* not because he fought physically, but because he didn't mind standing up for his principles and battling for what he knew to be right. He showed his ability as a leader by the way he dealt with bills in the state legislature.

Always fighting for the people, Tejeda passed laws as a state representative creating the Veteran's Housing Assistance Program. He helped improve the state's emergency medical system and passed legislation creating the Texas Crime Victim's Bill of Rights. Interested in children and families, he passed a law protecting the rights of children, the elderly, and the disabled.

He was sometimes called "squeaky clean" because he did not drink, smoke, or party. He also disapproved of gambling. Yet Tejeda was far from perfect. When asked what his worst fault was, he replied, "Probably having a quick temper. But I work on it and one of the things I have learned is to think before you act."

Tejeda never forgot that his roots were in San Antonio. During his sixteen years in the Texas Legislature, he kept strong ties with the people and the businesses that he represented. He learned how to work with other legislators, and to negotiate in a peaceful manner and not in anger.

In 1993 he was elected to the United States House of Representatives. He represented nine entire counties and parts of four more near the San Antonio area. He earned the respect of his fellow legislators as he served on the Armed Services Committee and Veteran's Affairs Committee. As a United States Congressman, he worked to make and pass laws in our nation's capital. His future as a leader in government seemed assured.

Yet Frank Tejeda's career was cut short. He became ill while in office with brain cancer. He had surgery and, with his usual courage, returned to work several weeks later. More treatment was required to try to stop the disease. Frank was determined to win this battle, as he had won so many in the past. But his health became worse. He was optimistic, but this was a fight he could not win. Congressman Tejeda died in January 1997. He left three children as survivors: Maria, Sonya, and Frank III.

Frank Tejeda served his state and his country, in war and in peace. His life was dedicated to the service of his country.

Jesse Treviño
ARTIST

When Jesse Treviño was in the first grade, he entered an art contest sponsored by the Witte Museum in San Antonio. Students were told to draw a wildlife scene. Jesse worked hard on his drawing, a picture of two doves on manila paper.

Jesse was present the day the museum announced the winners of the contest.

"I remember hearing my name called and walking to the podium to get the award, a plaque, and about $40. *This is what I want to do the rest of my life*, I thought."

At first it really seemed that his dreams would come true. He was a promising art student at Fox Technical High School in San Antonio. After graduation, he won a scholarship to the Art Students League in New York City. He was thrilled to be able to study under good teachers and become a professional artist. To help with expenses, he drew and sold portraits.

Then the Vietnam War began. His draft notice came, instructing Jesse to report for army duty. As a native of Mexico, he could have returned there and not served in the U.S. Army. But Jesse wanted to remain in the United States. Besides, his brothers had served in the war and survived. He went into the infantry.

Jesse Treviño

—Courtesy of Jesse Treviño

Jesse was with his platoon in the Mekong Delta of Vietnam when sniper bullets cut through the air. Many soldiers were hit—Jesse was shot in the arm, legs, and body. Unfortunately, his right arm was the one badly injured by gunfire.

After months in army hospitals in Vietnam and Japan, he returned to the United States. He spent two more years in Veterans' Hospitals, learning to walk again. A hook replaced his right hand. Jesse's mother, Mrs. Dolores Treviño, encouraged and supported her son as he tried to adjust to this terrible fate. The promising young artist had lost his painting arm—he knew he would never paint or sketch again.

He enrolled in San Antonio College but at first took no art classes. Then he took a life drawing class and learned how to use his left hand to draw. To his surprise, he received an "A" in the class. He realized he could still produce art with his left hand.

Jesse went on to earn his bachelor's degree at Our Lady of the Lake University, then his master's degree at University of Texas at San Antonio. While there he began taking photographs of his family and the neighborhood where he lived. He later used these photos as models for his paintings. He realized he wanted to paint the west side of San Antonio where he had grown up. He paid tribute to his Chicano roots and culture as he painted his brothers, his mother gathering laundry from the clothesline, and even the snow-cone vendor. His style could be called realistic because it shows the exact way people and buildings look. His interpretations of these local, much loved parts of his neighborhood made him something of a hero.

"Vietnam changed me," he said.

In 1994 Treviño's work earned a showing at the Smithsonian Institution's National Museum of American Art. Two of these paintings now hang in the Smithsonian Institution. "La Raspa" (the snow-cone vendor) and "Senora Dolores Treviño" (his mother in her back yard gathering laundry) are two of Treviño's most important works.

"Like many Chicano artists, I was interested in my roots. I experimented with a lot of different styles but finally decided to paint what was around me—what I had grown up with—the things that were about me, my family, my friends, my community," he told *Smithsonian* magazine.

Some of these paintings are in permanent collections of major corporations, including J.C. Penney, Dr. Pepper, and Anheuser-Busch. Prince Charles of England owns a painting, as does the former president of Mexico, Carlos Salinas de Gortari.

In 1995 he painted a mural for the San Antonio Central Library. The mural he painted at the library measures ten by thirty-six feet. Many symbols of San Antonio, such as movie marquees, bring back scenes of the old city. It reminds old-timers of San Antonio during World War II.

When Treviño was about thirty years old, he walked by the Santa Rosa Hospital in downtown San Antonio and stared at the bare, outside wall. He pictured in his mind a mural that would bring life and hope to the area. Much later the health care center for the hospital wanted a mural for the exterior wall and asked Jesse Treviño to create it.

Today, as visitors stand in the park across the street from the hospital, they see an enormous mural entitled "The Spirit of Healing." It is composed of more than 150,000 pieces of hand-cut ceramic tile, and may be the largest mural of its kind in North America. In the mural a broken-winged angel stands over a small child holding a dove. Bright red, orange, yellow, and purple tiles were used in the artwork which took three years to complete.

Treviño explained that using tiles, cutting them to fit a purpose, is a tradition in Mexico. He enlisted the help of local high school students to help him work on the construction in a warehouse on the west side of San Antonio. The ten students were paid to work twelve hours a week and received class credit.

What an opportunity that these students had in working with a professional artist! Some of them were at-risk students, but all worked hard and enjoyed the experience. One boy said he had thought of dropping out of school but now felt encouraged to stay.

Covering an area of forty feet by ninety feet, the mural looms high above the park and its surroundings. The boy is modeled after Treviño's own son. The broken wing of the angel symbolizes hurt and pain. Jesse knew these well as he lay bleeding in a rice paddy in Vietnam, wondering if he'd live or paint again. He feels that everyone has some hardship or tragedy to endure in life. The angel gives hope to those who suffer.

Santa Rosa Health Center is an important part of San Antonio's downtown. It is near the *mercado* and business district. It is Treviño's hope that his mural will bring people together. The director of support services at the health center, Fernando Martinez, said, "When folks come here because people or children are sick, they are going to sit and look at that mural and be inspired, and have a feeling of hope."

This hope may be healing the spirit as well as the body. Jesse Treviño knows how important it is for people to have hope. He overcame poverty as a child, the loss of his right hand and almost his life in Vietnam. Jesse Treviño knows about healing and the need for hope. He is still creating, selling, and displaying his work at many art galleries.

Vicente Villa
SCIENTIST AND PROFESSOR

Dr. Villa waves his arms and glides across the floor as he teaches. No, he's not teaching a dance step. He's teaching biology. "When you lecture on the amoeba, you must imitate an amoeba," he says.

With a touch of the actor, he speaks with animation and is rarely still. His classes are never dull. Dr. Vicente Villa is the kind of teacher we all wish we'd had. He never tires of explaining something new, uses dramatic ways to explain his subject, and gives you a big smile when you understand. He might even clap his hands or jump up and down and shout for joy!

His parents had little education but believed it was the key to success. They encouraged their children to go to school and get as much education as possible. Vicente Villa graduated from Laredo High School with math as his best subject. He did not take biology in high school. He was in junior college before he enrolled in his first biology course.

At the end of the first week of biology, he had read the entire book.

"I wanted to see how it ended," he says with a grin.

The instructor, Mr. Kelley, asked a question, and Vicente answered it in his thick, Spanish accent. Mr.

Dr. Vicente Villa

—Photo courtesy of
Southwestern University

Kelley was impressed that a student could already understand a difficult subject in such a short time. He smiled and praised the young man who barely spoke English. He continued to encourage him.

"That semester I fell in love with biology," Dr. Villa said. "Mr. Kelly fired me up because he cared, and I decided I wanted to study biology for the rest of my life."

Dr. Villa grew up in Laredo. His father was a *vaquero* early in life, then became a carpenter. His mother was almost blinded by an eye disease. His maternal grandmother was there for him, watching after him, even getting him small jobs when he was a boy.

The young Vicente always had some kind of job. He shined shoes for five cents a pair as he went door to door in the *barrios,* becoming street-wise as he did. He sold newspapers and even swept sidewalks. He always shared his pay with his family, which moved around in order for his father to find work. His mother loved to hear him read. When visitors came to their home, she often asked Vicente to read aloud. Later, when she eventually became blind, he read to her.

He still remembers experiences that had a positive effect on him. He was a Boy Scout and very involved in the group. He was also in the Boys Club of America.

Dr. Villa went on to complete a bachelor of science degree at the University of Texas at Austin. He spent many more hours than required in biology lab and worked hard in other classes. His biology professor admired his dedication and asked Vicente if he worked hard in his other subjects.

"Oh yes, I love biology and science."

"What do you plan to do after graduation?" Dr. Harold Bolden asked him.

"I want to teach high school biology," he replied.

"No, you will get a Ph.D. and teach at the college level," the professor said with certainty in his voice.

He spoke to Vicente but a few moments. Yet the time and interest he took had a big influence on the student's life. He knew he was valued and capable of achieving.

Vicente listened but was afraid he could not reach that goal. It would take more years of study in a university and research. How would he pay for it? Just before graduation, he married his childhood sweetheart, Alicia. He took a job teaching junior high school science. He enjoyed teaching but remembered what his professor and mentor had said to him. After talking it over with his wife, he decided to begin studying toward a higher degree and was able to get a scholarship for his studies. After several years of study and research, he received the degree from Rice University.

His first job after getting his Ph.D. was at New Mexico State University. He met Hispanic students there and, to help those with language difficulty, taught "Principios of Biologia" (in Spanish) at the university.

Dr. Villa realized his talent for teaching. He was named the best science teacher at New Mexico State University, then the best science teacher from all universities in New Mexico.

In 1985 Southwestern University in Georgetown recruited him to teach biology. Since that year he has been at Southwestern happily using his skills for teaching and mentoring. His courses are difficult, but Dr. Villa is always there to give extra help when needed. Some students might shy away from such courses as micro- or molecular biology, but Dr. Villa won't let them. Since his arrival in 1985, ten percent of biology majors at Southwestern are Hispanic. His students who have gone to medical school have achieved excellent ratings, and many are respected doctors now. He tries to be a mentor, a wise confidant, and trustful teacher. He is generous with his time, often helping students after hours and on weekends. He has also been known to give a "wake-up" call to sudents so they will not miss a class.

"Be a scholar, I urge you. Do the extra things that makes this worthwhile," he proclaims, gesturing with his hands.

Besides teaching, Dr. Villa has been involved in specialized research in genetics, the science that studies how offspring inherit traits from their parents. Scientific research challenges him. He feels compelled to discover new ideas that will help mankind.

Dr. Villa enjoys working with students of all ages. He often conducts summer workshops for students in middle school. How exciting it is for him to introduce young people to the subject he loves—biology.

In 1993 Dr. Villa was named Professor of the Year by the Washington, D.C., Council for Advancement and Support of Education. He won the award in competition with over 400 other professors from all over the United States. Dr. Villa was chosen for his commitment to teaching and his success in helping students achieve. Many students, past and present, made statements saying that he was the most dynamic and caring professor they have ever had. For over thirty years Dr. Villa has been teaching and mentoring students. He feels it is important to know each student and help them realize their goals. He is quick to give credit to his own teachers, beginning with Mr. Kelley in junior college, and then to his professors at U.T. and at Rice.

"I was so fortunate to have had such supportive teachers who believed in me."

Dr. Villa, along with the president of Southwestern University, went to Washington, D.C., for the award presentation by President Clinton. Dr. Villa received a sum of $10,000 and the opportunity to give a lecture at the Smithsonian Institution.

Of all his honors, Dr. Villa feels receiving this award

was the most important one of his career. He remembers the day when he walked into the White House.

"When I went to the White House to accept the award, we walked into the Oval Office of the president of the United States. As I walked in, what came to mind was that little shoeshine boy in Laredo. What a distance I have come," he says, his eyes misting.

Judith Zaffirini
TEXAS SENATOR

Judith Zaffirini represents Laredo and the surrounding areas near Mexico. She also represents Bexar County, which includes San Antonio. She takes her job as senator seriously, regarding it a privilege to serve the citizens of Texas and help pass laws that will help many people.

Senator Zaffirini grew up in Laredo in a warm, loving family with her parents and two sisters. She remembers attending the weekly storytelling hour at the local library as a reward for good behavior. At the public library she became aware of the world of books that would forever entertain and enlighten her.

"I discovered a passion for books that would last a lifetime," she says.

Reading was an important part of her childhood. She can still recall hearing her mother and dad reading to her. She especially enjoyed the *Raggedy Ann and Andy* books, the *Nancy Drew* mysteries, and in high school, *The Scarlet Pimpernel*.

"My first memory is of learning to read at my mother's side. My mother read stories and made up captions for the photographs."

The future senator had other interests as well. She

Judith Zaffirini
—Photo courtesy Senate Media Services

was head cheerleader at Ursuline Academy in Laredo and organized the city's first dance team to perform at football games. In elementary school she went from door to door selling peanuts for the March of Dimes. In high school she helped raise money for retarded children. Judith learned discipline and character at the Catholic schools she attended.

Always interested in government, she became president of her high school student council and the All-City Student Council. It is no surprise then that Judith Zaffirini wanted to be part of state government. She wanted to represent citizens near the Mexican border and help pass fair laws for all citizens of Texas.

Senator Zaffirini has a bachelor of science degree, master of arts, and Ph.D. degree from the University of Texas at Austin. She is active in the Blessed Sacrament Catholic Church. She is a true American with roots in several different ethnic groups. Her grandfather on her father's side came to Laredo from Greece and married a Hispanic woman. Her husband's grandfather came from Italy to Laredo and married a Hispanic woman. The families united when Judith and her husband, Carlos, married. They have one son, Carlos, Jr.

Before she ran for the state senate, she was well-known in the Democratic Party. Zaffirini had been active at all levels: local, district, state, and national. She had been vice chairwoman of the Texas Democratic Party and on the Executive Committee of the National Association of State Districts. She was urged by her fellow Democrats to run for the state senate.

She has served her district well and is devoted to speaking for citizens, especially those who live near the border of Mexico. At the top of her list of concerns are health, human services, and education issues that affect the elderly, children, and the disabled. She has passed 289 bills important in all for children and adults alike.

She worked to crack down on selling tobacco to minors, raised standards for nursing homes, and made health insurance possible for many people. She passed a bill to immunize one hundred percent of the children in our state. Children no longer have to have certain diseases if they get shots to prevent the disease.

One of her recent bills was another to help children. In 1997 Senator Zaffirini presented a bill to the state legislature to allow certain children to be adopted. If parents have abused or neglected their children, these children can now have permanent homes with loving adoptive parents. They no longer have to wait years for a good home.

She is the only senator who has a one hundred percent attendance record in the state legislature. She believes strongly that her votes speak for the people she represents. She feels she has a duty and responsibility. Senator Zaffirini hopes that her example will be noted by young people; they too can realize the importance of being responsible, present, and on time.

When Senator Zaffirini is not in session in the State Capitol at Austin working for the people, she works in Laredo. She owns Zaffirini Communications Co. This business provides communication services, including consultation, workshops, and seminars to coach people in public speaking and giving keynote addresses. The senator herself has had more than twenty years of public speaking experience. No wonder she is so successful in presenting her views and passing bills in the senate.

She has received over 300 honors and awards for her service in the state. *Texas Monthly* magazine named her one of the best state legislators of 1997. The South Texas Press Association honored her for her career in journalism and public service. The Texas Classroom Teachers Association named her Friend of Education.

To relax in her busy schedule, Judith likes to cook

for family and friends. She enjoys sports, especially watching her son play basketball.

Asked what she would like to say to students, she said, "I encourage students to do their best, stay in school, stay away from drugs and dream high."

Bibliography

Irma Aguilar
Smith, Jenni. "From home to school to work to school . . ." *Houston Chronicle,* September 6, 1998.
Texas Tech University Health Sciences Center.
Curriculum Vita of Irma Aguilar.
Interview with Irma Aguilar by Sammye Munson.

Vikki Carr
Machamer, Gene. *Hispanic American Profiles.* New York: Ballentine Books, 1996.
Meier, Matt. *Notable Latino Americans.* Connecticut: Greenwood Publishing, 1997.
Telgen, Diane and Jim Kamp, eds. *Notable Hispanic American Women.* Detroit: Gale Research Publications, 1993.
Personal biography of Vikki Carr.
Interview with Vikki Carr.
Live concert in Galveston, Texas.

Hector Galan
Chicano! History of the Mexican American Civil Rights Movement. Aired as PBS series, April 1996.
"Filmmaker Galan." *Austin American Statesman,* November 9, 1996.
Galan Productions website, October 3, 1997.
Morthland, John. "Border Music." *Texas Monthly,* September 1995.
Salas, Abel. "Filmmaker Hector Galan on Top of Documentary World." *Arriba,* March 11, 1994.
Internet interview with Hector Galan.

Carmen Lomas Garza
Children's Book Press. Biography of Carmen Lomas Garza.

Garza, Carmen Lomas. *In My Family,* 1996.
"Garza brings home art, art home." *Beeville Bee-Picayune,* February 5, 1992.
North Texas Institute for Educators on the Visual Arts. "Carmen Lomas Garza."
Olesson, J. R. *Austin American Statesman,* November 9, 1991.

Eligio (Kika) de la Garza
Arrillaga, Pauline. "Longtime lawmaker won't seek re-election." *Austin American Statesman,* December 9, 1995.
"Congressman Kika de la Garza Announces for Re-election." *Pharr Press,* February 25, 1976.
"De la Garza Gaining Respect in Washington." *Laredo Morning Times,* February 19, 1989.
Garrison, Gary. "LBJ, Others Honor Solon." *Austin American Statesman,* September 22, 1971.
Klinefelter, Karen. "Congressman Compiles Go-Go Guide." *Dallas News,* December 29, 1965.
Richards, Charles. "De la Garza seeks farm bill input." *Fort Worth Telegram,* April 19, 1981.
Riley, Jennifer. "De la Garza reflects on his long career." *Hispanic,* December 1996.
Sinclair, Ward. "The Man Called Kika." *Los Angeles Times,* January 1, 1983.
Telephone interview with Kika de la Garza.

Tish Hinojosa
Beal, Jim. "Songwriter Hinojosa Returns to the Roots." *San Antonio Express,* May 15, 1996.
Cada Nina, recording, Rounder Record Company, 1996.
Cosin, Elizabeth. "Tish Hinojosa Keeps on Rolling in Quest to Popularize her Latin folk-country music." *Los Angeles Daily News,* June 12, 1996.
Hinojosa, Tish, a biography, 1997.
"Hinojosa Embraces the Cultures." *Los Angeles Times,* 1994.
Kenling, Don. "Hinojosa Brings Bit of Southwest to Berwyn." *Chicago Times,* February 2, 1993.
Skanse, Richard. "Hinojosa's Homecoming." *San Antonio Current,* May 16, 1996.
"Tish Hinojosa Sings at Heaven's Gate." *Washington Post,* May 15, 1994.
U.S.A. Today. May 28, 1996.
Young, Ron. "West Side." *San Antonio Express News,* May 15, 1996.
Live concert, Houston, Texas. August 1998.

Conversation with Tish Hinojosa. August 1996.

Luis Jiménez
Anaya, Rodolfo et al. "Man on Fire: Luis Jiménez." Albuquerque Museum Catalog, University of New Mexico Press.
Ennis, Michael. "Luis Jiménez." *Texas Monthly,* September 1998.
Huerto, Benito. "Working Class Heroes." *Images from the Popular Culture, Exhibits, U.S.A.*
Kirr, Susan. "Recasting the Icons of the West." *Texas Highways,* August 1998.
Laguna Gloria Art Museum notes, 1983.
Lippard, Lucy. "Dancing with History." The Albuquerque Museum, *University of New Mexico Press,* 1994.
Comments in writing from Luis Jiménez to Sammye Munson.

Linda Sagarnaga Magill
Hernandez, Blanca. "Helping Hands." *Houston Post Viva,* February 4, 1994.
Interview with Linda Sagarnaga Magill by Sammye Munson.

Pat Mora
Beacon Press, 1998. Biographical material.
McDougall Littell, Inc., 1999. Biography and "Conversation with Pat Mora," Electronic.
Mora, Pat. *Aunt Carmen's Book of Practical Saints.* Boston: Beacon Press, 1997.
Mora, Pat. *A Birthday Basket for Tia.* New York: Simon and Schuster, MacMillan Press, 1992.
Mora, Pat. *Confetti Poems for Children.* New York: Lee and Low, 1996.
Mora, Pat. *House of Houses.* Boston: Beacon Press, 1997.
Mora, Pat. *This Big Sky.* New York: Scholastic Books, 1998.
Mora, Pat. *Tomás and the Library Lady.* New York: Knopf, 1989.
Publishers' Weekly. Review of *House of Houses,* March 24, 1997.
Racine, Marty. "Border Voices." *Houston Chronicle,* May 30, 1999.

Dan Morales
Draper, Robert. "Dan Morales." *Texas Monthly,* September 1996.
Duff, Audrey. "Dan Morales." *Current,* October 6, 1994.
Garcia, James. "Rising Star in Lone Star State." *San Antonio Express Vista,* February 17, 1997.
Garcia, James. "Morales Seems Likely to Become a Colonial Czar in S. Texas." *Austin American Statesman,* July 26, 1996.

Ganino, Denise. "Attorney General Morales." *Austin American Statesman,* February 9, 1997.
Kilday, Anne Marie and Jonathan Eig. "Psychiatric Hospital Settles Lawsuit." *Dallas Morning News,* June 3, 1992.
McNeely, Dave. "Morales Lagging Despite Best Intentions." *Austin American Statesman,* September 24, 1995.
Morales, Dan. Biography and letter. 1998.
"Morales Takes Hopwood Heat." *Hispanic Journal,* April 1997.
"The Morales Brief on Tobacco Money." *Austin American Statesman,* February 1, 1998.
"What Makes Morales Take on Tobacco?" *Austin American Statesman,* August 18, 1996.

Guadalupe Quintanilla
King, Fred. "Civil Rights Nominee Fought to Succeed." *Houston Post,* May 22, 1982.
Wade, Mary D. *Guadalupe Quintanilla: Leader of Hispanic Community.* New Jersey: Enslow Publishing, 1995.
Interview with Guadalupe Quintanilla.

Hilda Tagle
"Confirmed At Last." *Corpus Christi Caller Times,* March 14, 1998.
Day, Jim. "A Winding Road for Tagle, from Beauty School to Federal Judge." *Corpus Christi Caller Times,* March 25, 1998.
Garland, William. "Tagle renominated for federal Judgeship." *Corpus Christi Caller Times,* March 22, 1997.
George, Ron. "Judgeship Heavy for Tagle." *Corpus Christi Caller Times.*
Guerro, Carlos. "Beauty Shop to Bench." *Austin American Statesman,* April 4, 1998.
Hernandez, Anissa. "Bravo-Judge Tagle on New Appointment." *La Onda,* April 4, 1998.
Lawrence, Guy. "Judge H. Tagle's Hometown Pays Tribute with Parade." *Corpus Christi Caller Times,* June 21, 1998.
O'Connell, Jim. "Tagle's Bid for Judge Advances." *Corpus Christi Caller Times,* February 26, 1998.
Rivera, Anissa. "Judge H. Tagle Celebrates 50th Birthday." *La Onda,* Enero, 1997.
"Senate Holdup." *Corpus Christi Caller Times,* October 7, 1996.

Frank Tejeda
Congressional Quarterly Weekly Report, January 16, 1993.
McDonald, Gregg. "Tribute Paid to a Quiet Warrior." *Houston Chronicle,* February 9, 1997.

Phelan, Craig. "Dossier." *San Antonio Express News,* August 12, 1984.
Robison, Clay. "Solon a Part of His Roots." *San Antonio Light,* April 10, 1977.
Thomas, Robert. "Tejeda, 51, Congressman From Texas and Former Marine." *Houston Chronicle,* February 9, 1997.

Jesse Treviño
Allen, Paula. "Portraits of Life in the City." *San Antonio Express News,* March 27, 1994.
Bennett, Steve. "Muralist." *San Antonio Express News,* September 17, 1995.
Brown, Chip. "Artist's Mural Inspires Hope for Healing Bodies and Souls." *Houston Chronicle,* October 12, 1997.
Goddard, Dan. "Texas Artist's Work in National Museum." *San Antonio Express News,* September 18, 1994.
"Highlights." *Smithsonian,* December 1994.
Pierce, Ellise. "Spirit of Healing." *Texas Journey,* January-February, 1998.
Salas, Abell. "Arts Veteran." *Hispanic Magazine,* Septemer 1997.

Vicente Villa
"Carski Foundation Distinguished Teaching Award." *American Society for Microbiology,* April 1996.
"Educator Has Teaching Down to a Science." *Dallas Morning News,* September 21, 1993.
Fisher, Mark. "Sphere of Influence." *Council for Advancement for the Support of Education,* January 1994.
Ling, Brenda. "A Top Professor's Winning Dedication." *USA Today,* September 21, 1993.
Smith, Sarita. "La Voz de Barrio." *Austin American Statesman,* September 21, 1993.
"Villa Named Professor of the Year." *Southwestern,* Fall 1993.
Interview with Dr. Vicente Villa, 1998.

Judith Zaffirini
Fikac, Peggy. "Senate OKs Legislation to expedite Adoption." *Austin American Statesman,* April 9, 1997.
Telgren, Diane and Jim Kamp, eds. *Notable Hispanic American Women.* Detroit: Gale Research, 1993.
"The Best State Legislators." *Texas Monthly,* July 1997.
"Zaffirini Announces Candidacy." *Beeville-Bee Picayune,* December 1995.
Biography and letter from Judith Zaffirini, 1998.

F
395
.M5
M88
2000